## Hey, listen to this!

What did the baby porcupine say when it
   backed into the cactus?
*Is that you, Mother?*

Everybody likes a good joke, but the same
story that sends one person into hysterical
laughter may leave someone else staring
at the wall, whistling under his breath. In
this collection of jokes and jests from our
folklore there's something to make everybody laugh, along with some good ex-
planations about what humor is and why
we find it funny.

There are jokes based on wild exaggerations, and others on punning of every
kind. There are catch riddles with impossible answers. There are tales of foolish
behavior with roots centuries old. And
there are shaggy dog stories that are just
plain foolish. Tom Swifties, Confucius
Say jokes, and other old friends are here
too. Alvin Schwartz also includes in this
collection a number of the "hate" jokes,
"in" jokes, and "cruel" or "sick" jokes we
tell one another, explaining what purpose
they serve.

There are an enormous number of jokes
in circulation today. Most have no known
authors. Like games and songs and other

# Witcracks

W hen you . . . laugh open your mouth wide enough for the noise to get out without squealing, throw your head back as though you was going to get shaved, hold on to your false hair with both hands and then laugh until your soul gets thoroughly rested.

—Josh Billings

# Witcracks
## JOKES AND JESTS
## FROM AMERICAN FOLKLORE

Collected by ALVIN SCHWARTZ
Illustrated by GLEN ROUNDS

J. B. Lippincott Company
Philadelphia and New York

U. S. Library of Congress Cataloging in Publication Data

Schwartz, Alvin, birth date       comp.
   Witcracks: jokes and jests from American folklore.
   SUMMARY: Traces the history and gives examples of
puns, shaggy dog stories, and other jokes from American
humor of the nineteenth and twentieth centuries.
   Bibliography: p.
   1. American wit and humor.   2. Wit and humor, Juvenile.
[1. American wit and humor.   2. Joke books]   I. Rounds,
Glen, birth date       illus. II. Title.
PN6162.S33              817′.008              73-7630
ISBN-0-397-31475-2      ISBN-0-397-31476-0  (pbk.)

"So muddy" (p. 21), "Willie fell" (p. 84) reprinted from *The Humor of Humor,* Evan Esar, copyright 1952, by permission of the publisher, Horizon Press, New York. "Boobee" (p. 32), "Little old lady," (p. 38), "Dishes," (p. 39), "So long" (p. 51), "bake cookies" (p. 86) copyright © 1959, 1963 by the California Folklore Society. Reprinted from *Western Folklore,* vol. 22, pp. 250–254; vol. 18, p. 180; vol. 22, p. 151, by permission of the Society. "Sneakers" (p. 41) reprinted by permission from TIME, The Weekly Newsmagazine, Aug. 2, 1963, p. 41. Copyright © Time, Inc.

"Pressing engagement," "the end" (p. 50) reprinted from *Journal of American Folklore,* vol. 69, pp. 115–122, by permission of American Folklore Society and Herbert Halpert. Copyright © by American Folklore Society, 1956. "Chemist" (p. 52) reprinted by permission from *Senior Scholastic.* "I weighed" (p. 62), "a crew" (p. 64) reprinted by permission from *Esquire Magazine,* Sept., 1943, pp. 32, 54. Copyright 1943 (renewed 1971) by Esquire, Inc. "One day a man" (p. 92) reprinted by permission

For Peter

# Contents

# Listen to this!

When a boy I know tells a joke he usually starts by saying, "Hey, listen to this!" And usually I stop and listen, for he has a kooky sense of humor I like, and he tells good jokes.

Of course, the problem in telling jokes is always the same. Will your audience laugh? Or will they stare at you as if you are slightly odd? No one knows until he tries.

Actually, most of the jokes we tell are concerned with two things. One is what is happening around us. The other is how people behave.

We tell many for the fun of it, asking only that someone laugh. But curiously we tell many others in anger. For we also use jokes to ridicule people and things we don't like, which helps us to let off steam.

In every case we tell jokes the way people always have. We weave them into tales. We build them around puns. We wrap them in riddles and rhymes.

There are these days enormous numbers of jokes roaming the land. But most of them have no authors.

As with games and songs and other folklore, they appear out of nowhere, often disappear, then at times reappear in new forms. As a result, some are very old, despite their modern dress.

So listen to this!

Alvin Schwartz

Princeton, New Jersey

# Witcracks

# 1.

## Last winter a cow nearby caught such a cold she gave nothing but ice cream.

This is, of course, a lie. And so is everything else in this chapter. But the lies you will find are not ordinary ones. They are big outlandish exaggerations conjured up years ago for the fun of it.

Each involves only a few words, but they are funny because they are so ridiculous. Folklorists call them Yankeeisms or Jonathanisms.

"Brother Jonathan," for whom they are named, was a make-believe country boy, an awkward, gawky, gangling fellow. In the early 1800s he was briefly the national symbol of the United States, much as Uncle Sam is today.

In Jonathan's day outlandish lies were the most popular kind of humor. If you use them, do it right. Look your listener straight in the eye. And don't smile, although that will be harder than you think.

There is a man in this town who is so tall he has to stand on a ladder to shave himself. In fact, he has to get on his knees just to put his hands in his pockets.

When he was born he was so big it was impossible to name all of him at once.

He has a son who is growing so fast his shadow can't keep up with him. Nor can his clothes. One day his head grew three inches through the top of his hat.

There is a man nearby whose feet are so large that when it rains he lies down and uses them as umbrellas. And when the sun is too hot he does the same thing to provide some shade.

Not too far from here there is a farmer who is so strong that when his horse fell in a well, he dug up the whole thing and gently poured him out.

He has a wife who is so clean that one day she scrubbed the kitchen floor too hard and went right through into the basement.

But it is their farm that is the problem.

It is so muddy they have to jack up the cows to milk them.

There is also a family in this town that is so lazy it takes two of them to sneeze. One throws his head back. And another goes AH-CHOO!

It also takes two of them to chop wood. One swings the ax. And another grunts.

There is a man not too far away who is so dirty that when he finally took a bath, he found some underwear he thought he had lost two years before.

There is also a man who is so forgetful that one night
he put his cat to bed and put himself outside. He did
not discover his mistake until a dog chased him and he
found he could not climb a tree.

Another time he put his best shirt to bed
    and sent himself to the laundry to be washed.
But he didn't realize what he had done
    until they tried to iron him.




There is also this woman who is so smart
    it hurts to think about it.
Each night she fries herself a giant buckwheat cake,
    then rushes it sizzling hot to her bed where she uses it
    as a blanket.
Then each morning on arising she eats it for breakfast.

# 2.

## What is yellow,
## smooth,
## and deadly?

True riddles are word puzzles you may be able to solve if you put your mind to it. But riddles like the one above are impossible to solve because the answer is a trick and a joke.

In some cases it is the words that fool you. You expect them to mean one thing and they mean another. In other cases, it is the sounds they make. For instance:

Why can one never starve in a desert?
*Because of the sand which is there.*

Riddles like these, whose answers are puns, are called conundrums. Some of them are very old. Today we also use riddles which depend on nothing but nonsense.

What *is* yellow, smooth, and deadly?
*Shark-infested custard, of course.*

Why is that dog running in circles?
*It's a watchdog, and it's winding itself up.*

Why did your cat join the Red Cross?
*It wants to be a first aid kit.*

What did the five-hundred-pound mouse say when it walked into the alley?

*Here, kitty, kitty, kitty!*

Why does the baby duck walk softly?
*Because it's a baby and it can't walk, hardly.*

Why does a cow wear a bell?
*Its horns don't work.*

What did the cow ask the silo?
*Is my fodder in there?*

What did the baby porcupine say when
it backed into the cactus?

*Is that you, Mother?*

What is a boobee?
*A little bug that runs up the leg of a bee*
*and yells:*

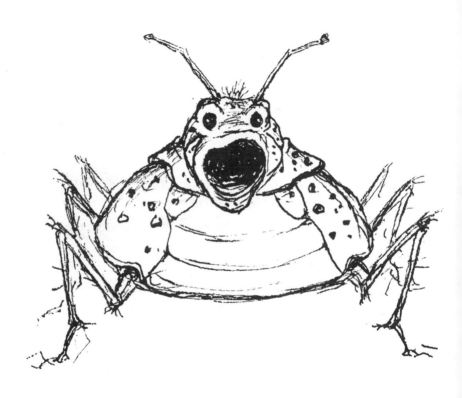

**BOO**, bee!

What did the
   angry octopus
say to the
   octopus
that made him
   angry?
*One of these*
   *days,*
   *pow*
   *pow*
   *pow*
   *pow*
   *pow*
   *pow*
   *pow*
   *pow—*
*right in the*
   *kisser!*

What did one eye say to the other?
*There's something between us that smells.*


What did one toe say to the other?
*Don't look now, but there's a heel following us.*


What do you do if you smash your toe?
*You call a tow truck.*

What is black and shiny and lives in trees
　　and is dangerous?
*A crow with a submachine gun.*

What is a ringleader?

*The first one in a bathtub.*

And what is a meat thief?
*A hamburglar.*

And a bulldozer?
*A sleeping bull.*

And rhubarb?
*Celery with high blood pressure.*

And ignorance?
*When you don't know something and*
*somebody finds out.*

Knock, knock!
*Who's there?*
Little old lady.
*Little old lady who?*
I didn't know
you could yodel.

"Knock, knock" riddles became popular in the early 1930s. In those days it was against the law in the United States to use alcoholic beverages. As a result, millions of people did their drinking in secret taverns called speakeasies.

To get into a speakeasy one usually had to knock on a locked door, then identify himself. Which is, more or less, where these riddles came from and how they work.

Knock, knock!
*Who's there?*
Cantaloupe.
*Cantaloupe who?*
We cantaloupe tonight. My father's watching.


Knock, knock!
*Who's there?*
Adolph.
*Adolph who?*
Adolph ball hit me in de mowf.
Dat's why I dawk dis way.


Knock, knock!
*Who's there?*
Sara.
*Sara who?*
Sara doctor in the house?


Knock, knock!
*Who's there?*
Dishes.
*Dishes who?*
Dishes me. Who ish you?

No one can explain for certain where they came from, or why, but in 1962 and 1963 great herds of elephant riddles began clomping across the country. And they still are seen and heard.

Why does an elephant have a trunk?
*So that it has someplace to hide when*
   *it sees a mouse.*

Why does it have tusks?
*Usually its parents can't afford braces.*

Why does it like peanuts?
*It can send in the wrappers for prizes.*

What is big and green and has a trunk?
*An unripe elephant.*

Why does an elephant wear sneakers?
*To sneak up on mice.*


What goes clomp, clomp, clomp, swish?
*An elephant with wet sneakers.*

Why does an elephant paint himself red?
*Why?*
So he can hide in a cherry tree.
*Have you ever seen an elephant in a cherry tree?*
No. See how effective it is?


How does an elephant get into a cherry tree?
*He sits on a seed and waits.*


How does he get out?
*He sits on a leaf and waits until fall.*

How can you tell when an elephant is under your bed?

*Your nose hits the ceiling.*

What is the best way to get out from
    under an elephant?
*Wait until he goes away.*

How do you stop a herd of elephants
    from charging?
*You take away their credit cards.*

Why do elephants wear short pants?
*You would too if you lived in
    that hot jungle.*

Why do elephants wear sunglasses?
*So that nobody will recognize them.*

# 3.

## I bought a wooden whistle,
## but it wooden whistle.

The last chapter had many riddles whose answers were puns. This chapter has many puns, but no riddles. Like many writing men, the famous author Oliver Wendell Holmes was a pun-hater. "He who makes a pun will pick a pocket," he warned. Don't you believe it!

"This is r-r-r-rough!"
  said the dog
  as he slid on the gravel.

"This can't be beat!"
  said the farmer
  as he pulled up a carrot.

Such expressions are called Wellerisms. They start with a common saying, then end in a way nobody expects. People have been fooling with them for two thousand years and more. But they have had a name only since the 1830s, when Charles Dickens created a character named Sam Weller who forever was using Wellerims. Here are some others.

"I believe in getting to the bottom of things,"
  said the father
  as he spanked his sassy son.

"I'm all in,"
　　said the burglar
　　as he wriggled through the window.


"I have a pressing engagement,"
　　said the man
　　as he took his pants to the cleaners.


"This is the end,"
　　said the little boy
　　as his pants fell off.

"So

long!"

said

the

chimp

as

he

slid

down

the

giraffe's

neck.

When China faced serious problems twenty-five hundred years ago, a wise man named Confucius gave advice on what to do. When the United States faced serious problems in the 1930s, many wise men offered many ideas on what to do. In those years Confucius became the hero of a series, or cycle, of jokes in which he poked fun at all this advice.

*Confucius say,*
> "Man who put face in punch bowl get punch in nose."

> "Chemist who fall in acid get absorbed in work."

> "Man who live in glass house should dress in basement."

> "Place to look for helping hand is end of own arm."

*Confucius also say,*
  "Man who put foot in mouth . . .

get athlete's tongue."

In 1910 appeared the first of forty books on the adventures of a businesslike young man named Tom Swift. In 1953 appeared the first of fifty on Tom, Jr., who was just as businesslike. Soon after appeared a vast number of businesslike puns called Tom Swifties. . . .

"I'll have four hot dogs,"
said Tom frank-ly.

"I have just inherited a million dollars,"
said Tom fortune-ately.

"I'll have two sodas,"
said Tom Cokes-ingly.

"What vegetable goes with carrots?"
asked Tom peas-fully.

"Whoops! I've dropped the eggs,"
Tom cracked.

"Please pass the sugar,"
said Tom sweetly.

"I don't have a penny left,"
said Tom in-no-cent-ly.

Have you heard
   about Will Knott?
He is so lazy
   he signs his name

*Won't*

I bought
a wooden
whistle,
but it
wooden
whistle.
I bought
a steel
whistle,
but it
steel
wooden
whistle.
So
I bought
a tin
whistle.
And now
I tin
whistle!

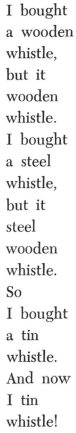

# 4.

## "I snored so loud
## I used to wake myself up."

"What did you do about it?" the listener asks.
"I cured myself."
"How?"
"Now I sleep in the next room and don't hear a thing."

This is one of countless noodle or numskull tales about the foolish ways people behave. They have been told for centuries everywhere.

Since the 1940s most American noodle tales have had as their "heroes" people called Little Morons. Their silly blunders and curious behavior fill this chapter.

This house painter was on a ladder and his partner was down below.

"Hey, you got a firm grip on that brush?" the one below called up.

"Yup!" the one above called down.

"Okay. Hang on. I need the ladder."

"I weighed only three pounds when I was born,"
  the man said.
"Did you live?" his friend asked.
"Did I live? You should see me now!"


"I'm really glad you named me Egbert,"
  the boy told his mother.
"Why?" she asked.
"That's what all the kids at school call me."


This woman's son was away in the army and he wrote
her that he had grown another foot. And she knit him
another sock.

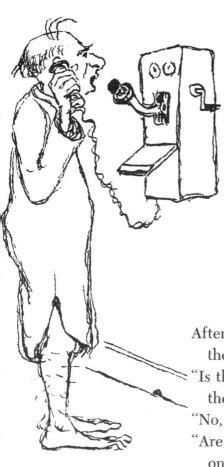

After everyone was in bed
the telephone rang.
"Is this one one one one?"
the voice asked.
"No, this is eleven eleven."
"Are you sure this isn't
one one one one?"
"Yes, I'm sure. This is
eleven eleven."
"Well, sorry to have gotten
you up."
"That's all right. I had to
get up anyway. The phone was
ringing."

A crew of workmen was building a house. After a lot of activity the one in charge went over to see the boss.

"Say," he asked, "did you want this house built from the top down or from the bottom up?"

"Why, from the bottom up," the boss said.

"Well, okay," he sighed. Then he turned and yelled, "Tear 'er down, boys! We gotta start over!"

*Have you heard about these people?*

The man who threw his shoes away because he thought they were sticking their tongues out at him.

The girl who went to the corner to see the traffic jam. A truck came along and gave her a jar.

The boy who sat in the living room because he thought he was dying.

The family who moved to the city because they heard the country was at war.

The boy who thought he was a magician. He went around the corner and turned into a drug store.

The girl who was so bashful she went into a closet to change her mind.

The football player who asked his coach to flood the field so he could go in as a sub.

The man who went to a football game because he thought a quarterback was a refund.

The man who wore a winter coat to a baseball game because he heard thousands of fans would be there.

The girl who tied her shoelaces in a most peculiar way.

A boy and his father are walking through a forest. The boy has his hands cupped together.

"What do you have in there?" his father asks.

"What do you think?" the boy asks back.
"Is it a rock?"
"No."
"Is it a flower?"
"No."
"Is it a bird?"
"No."
"Is it a horse?"
The boy opens his hands a little and peeks inside.
"What color?"

Why did the girl put her bed in the fireplace?
She wanted to sleep like a log.

Three boys were sharing the same bed. But it was so crowded one got out and tried to sleep on the floor. After a while one of his friends told him he might as well come back.

"There's lots more room now," he said.

# 5.

## Ahs your new neighbor.

The jokes in the last chapter made fun of foolish behavior. But they were gentle, good-natured jokes. Those in this chapter are "hate" jokes which grow out of conflicts between different groups.

Many people use these jokes as weapons to put down blacks, Puerto Ricans, Polish-Americans, Italian-Americans, and other minorities who compete with them for jobs and housing.

As might be expected, these groups strike back with jokes which also are angry and insulting.

Most of us tell such jokes only to our friends. What is curious, however, is that hate jokes are among the ones we tell most often. It has always been this way.

Since the same angry, insulting jokes are used against many groups, you will find blanks instead of names in the examples below.

Why do flies have wings?
To beat the _____s to the garbage dump.

Why do the _____s wear pointed shoes?
To get at the cockroaches in the corners.

Why don't they let the _____s swim in the harbor?
They would leave a ring around it.

Who is the bridegroom at a _____ wedding?
He's the one with the clean T-shirt.

Why does it take three _____s to screw in a light bulb?
You need one to hold the bulb in place and two to turn
the ladder.

Why does it take one hundred and one _____s to paint
a house?
You need one to hold the brush and one hundred to turn
the house.

Why did the _____ lose his new job as an elevator op-
erator?
He couldn't learn the route.

Why are the mothers of _____s so strong?
From raising dumbbells.

Many jokes that members of minorities tell are like the ones here. But they also tell other jokes that outsiders seldom hear. These show not only their anger but their fear, despair, and hope. Since such jokes usually remain within a group, they are called "in" jokes.

Probably the best examples of "in" jokes are those that blacks tell one another about their relationships with whites.

Years ago Southern blacks told stories about how mean Southern whites were. They were so bad, they said, that in some states blacks couldn't drink white milk and in other states they couldn't put their black feet in white shoes.

These were exaggerations and caused much laughter. But they also were sad stories of frustration that told of freedom beyond reach.

When blacks began to struggle for equal rights, and at first got nowhere, a gruesome cartoon appeared at which many laughed loud and long. Yet whites who saw it found nothing funny.

The cartoon showed a sportsman's den in which were mounted the heads of animals he had killed. There were a deer's head, an elk's head, and a tiger's head. Along with these was the head of a black man.

Two young white boys were looking at the black man's head. Pointing to it, one said to the other, "My daddy got that one in Detroit last week."

As blacks saw it their situation was so bad all they could do was laugh. The black poet Langston Hughes called it "desperate laughter." Years earlier Abraham Lincoln explained this feeling in a similar way. "Don't you see," he said, "that if I didn't laugh I would have to weep?"

As blacks slowly began to win greater equality their jokes slowly began to change. There was this one, for example, about integration.

> Knock, knock!
> *Who's there?*
> Ahs.
> *Ahs who?*
> Ahs your new neighbor.

And there was this joke about the copilots of an airplane, one white, one black. Their plane developed engine trouble and it became clear that it was going to crash.

The white pilot shouted: "Well, I finally found a way to get rid of you. I never wanted you to be my copilot anyway, so I took just one parachute aboard."

But the black man was gone. From a distance came a voice growing fainter and fainter. "I know," it said, "I know. . . ."

In their struggle for equal rights, the American Indians have told similar jokes. One is about the Lone Ranger and his faithful Indian friend Tonto who, over the years on radio and TV, had fought evil of every kind.

Looking across the prairie one day the Lone Ranger saw what to him seemed a frightful sight.

"Good heavens, Tonto!" he said. "There are two thousand wild and maddened Indians swooping down over the prairie and only we are here to stop them!"

And Tonto replied, "What do you mean *we*, paleface?"

But not all "in" jokes are like these. Many are cheerful, yet also help bind a group together. For example:

What nine-letter word does a Jewish grandmother use most often when she talks to her grandchild? "Eateateat!"

Which means that the way Jewish grandmothers often show affection for their grandchildren is by stuffing them with food. Of course, most grandmothers do this. But the Jews have made a joke of it which they share and enjoy.

# 6.

## "Johnny, stop twisting
## your sister's head."

Three times Johnny's mother asks him to stop. But he pays no attention. Then finally she says, "All right, Johnny, give it back to her."

This is a "sick" or "cruel" joke, part of what is called the Comedy of Horror. Such jokes deal with the dreadful way some parents treat their children, the angry feelings some children have about brothers and sisters, the threat of a ghastly illness or a violent war, and other subjects which make us feel uncomfortable.

In telling jokes about such situations we make them seem less threatening. We also tell them for another reason. They shock our listeners, and we like the reaction.

When a Tennessee storyteller named Sut Lovingood gathered his tales into a book in the 1860s, he warned that they might not "sit purfeckly quiet ontu the stomacks ove sum pussons. . . ." This is true of the stories in this chapter. But we continue to tell them.

At the turn of the century a number of sick jokes involved an English boy named Billy who was the hero, or victim, of a book called *Ruthless Rhymes for Heartless Homes*. For example:

Billy in one of his nice new sashes *
Fell into the fire and was burned to ashes;
Now, although the room grows chilly,
I haven't the heart to poke poor Billy.

In the United States Billy became Little Willie and for over thirty years was the subject of thousands of ghastly rhymes.

Little Willie with a dreadful shout
Gouged the baby's eyeballs out.
And jumped on them and made them pop,
And Daddy said, "Willie, stop!"

And:

Willie fell down the elevator,
Wasn't found 'til six days later.
Then all the neighbors gagged and sniffed,
"Gee whiz! How spoilt that Willie is!"

---

* Many English children used to wear sashes around their waists.

After Little Willie came Little Audrey, a fun-loving girl who laughed and laughed at life's tragedies because she knew, even at her tender age, that there wasn't much she could do about them.

One day Little Audrey and her grandmother were watching a lot of trucks and steamrollers fixing the road in front of their house. Suddenly her grandmother saw a coin in the road.

"There's a quarter!" she shouted and ran to get it. As she stooped to pick it up, a steamroller came along and squashed her flat.

And Little Audrey laughed and laughed. She knew all along it wasn't a quarter, only a nickel.

Little Audrey also created tragedies of her own.

There was the time she took parachute lessons. When she was ready to make her first jump, her relatives from far and near came to watch for no one in the family ever had jumped from a plane.

But all the way down Little Audrey laughed and laughed. She knew she was going to fool her relatives because she wasn't wearing her parachute.

The adventures of Little Audrey were followed in the 1950s by completely different kinds of "cruel" jokes. They grew out of the great changes which were taking place and how anxious they made us feel about our lives.

Among the best known were those that attacked mean parents:

Why are we out in our boat tonight, Daddy?
*Just tie that cement block around your leg, okay?*

But I don't want to go to Europe, Mommy.
*Shut up, kid, and keep swimming.*

Mommy, why can't we get a garbage disposal?
*Shut up and start chewing.*

Mommy, Mommy, are you sure that's the way to bake cookies?
*Shut up and get back in the oven.*

Mommy, Mommy, why is Daddy running so fast?
*Shut up and reload!*

Still others were rooted in a fear that war would destroy us all. There was this story which became known as the World War III joke or the H-bomb joke:

Knock, knock!
*Who's there?*

There is no answer.

# 7.

# Kkluuge!

None of the tales in this chapter end the way you might expect. In every case, in fact, they let you down like a lead balloon. But they *are* funny.

They are called shaggy dog stories. No one is sure just why except that one of the most popular in recent years did involve a shaggy dog.

When the dog got lost, its owner, who lived in England, advertised far and wide. A man in the United States saw the ad and miraculously found a dog like the one that was missing. At great expense he took it to England, only to be told it was the wrong dog. "You see," he was informed, "ours wasn't *that* shaggy."

But stories like this were being told long before they had a name. Abraham Lincoln told them. So did Davy Crockett. And so did the ancient Greeks. And if you are nutty enough, so will you.

A city man named Smith was driving through the countryside when his car suddenly sputtered and rolled to a stop. "I've got plenty of gas," he thought, "so it must be the motor."

He lifted the hood and tinkered with this and that, but couldn't figure out what was wrong.

"The trouble is with the carburetor," a deep voice behind him said. But when he turned all he could see was a bull.

"Did, uh, did you, er, say something?" Smith asked.

"Yes," the bull replied. "I said the trouble is with the carburetor." Then he walked toward the car and peered under the hood.

Meanwhile, the man took off like a shot for a farmhouse down the road, where he told what had happened.

"Is this a big bull with a sort of floppy left ear?" the farmer asked.

"That's the one!"

"Well, I wouldn't pay much attention to him," the farmer said. "That bull, he doesn't know as much about cars as he thinks he does."

A reindeer walked into a snack shop, hopped up on a stool at the counter, and ordered a fifty-cent hot butterscotch sundae.

When it arrived he put a ten-dollar bill on the counter. But the waiter thought he wouldn't know anything about money and gave him only a dollar in change.

"You know," said the waiter, "we don't get many reindeer here. In fact, you're the first one we've ever had."

"Well," the reindeer replied, "at nine dollars a sundae you're not likely to get many more."

One day a man went shopping at a country fair for a good horse. He found what seemed to be a fine animal, but the dealer asked such a low price it made him suspicious.

"Is there anything wrong with this horse?" he asked.

"Well," said the dealer, "there is one small thing. He likes to sit on grapefruit. Whenever he sees one he hustles over and sits down on it and won't budge."

"Well, I don't see much grapefruit in these parts," the man said. "So I guess I'll buy him."

He paid for the horse, mounted up, and started for home. On the way they had to cross a stream, but right in the middle of it, with water all around, the horse sat down, and the man slid off.

"There must be a grapefruit in this stream," the man muttered to himself. First he looked under the horse, as best he could. Then he looked all around it. But he found nothing that looked anything like a grapefruit. However, the horse would not move.

Sopping wet, the man waded ashore and started back to the fair on foot. By the time he got there he was mad enough to eat horseshoes.

When he finally found the dealer who had sold him the horse, he bellowed, "You said the only thing wrong with that animal was that he sat on grapefruit. Right now he's sitting in the middle of a stream and there is no grapefruit! And he won't budge!"

"Oh, my goodness," said the dealer. "I forgot to tell you. He sits on fish, too."

There was this knight who was very brave, but a little strange. While all the other knights rode horses, he preferred to ride his faithful Great Dane.

One night while returning from a trip he was caught in a violent rainstorm and sought shelter at an inn. The innkeeper hated knights and refused to give him a room. But when he saw the dog standing there soaking wet, his heart softened.

"I couldn't turn a knight out on a dog like this," he said.

On this island lived a fisherman who each morning, rain or shine, would go to sea in his boat and catch what fish he could. And each night he excitedly would tell his family of the tremendous fish he had seen and had almost caught.

This fisherman had two sons of whom he was very proud. One was named Toward. And the other was named Away.

One morning he took his sons fishing with him for the first time. That night when he returned he was more excited than ever.

"Lucy," he told his wife, "you should have seen the tremendous monster of a fish we saw today. It was five feet long. And it had little legs like a caterpillar and crawled right up on the beach. But before I could do anything it grabbed Toward and swallowed him in one gulp."

"Oh, that's terrible," his wife said. "Oh, how awful! Oh, poor Toward!"

"But that's only part of it," he said holding his head. "You should have seen the one that got Away."

An elderly man who lived alone took his dinner each night in the same restaurant at the same table.

One night, after he had paid his bill and put on his hat, he walked up a wall, across the ceiling, down another wall, and out the door.

"That's odd," his waiter said. "Usually he says good night."

This is a story Mark Twain once told about an interview he had with a newspaper reporter.

"Isn't that a brother of yours?" the reporter asked, pointing to a portrait on the wall.

"Oh, yes, yes, yes!" he replied. "Now that you remind me of it, that *was* a brother of mine. That's Willie—*Bill* we called him. Poor old Bill!"

"Why? Is he dead, then?"

"Ah! Well, I suppose so. We never could tell. There was a great mystery about it."

"That is sad, very sad. He disappeared, then?"

"Well, yes, in a sort of general way. We buried him."

"*Buried* him! *Buried* him? Without knowing whether he was dead or not?"

"Oh, no! Not that. He was dead enough."

"Well . . . if you buried him, and you knew he was dead—"

"No! No! We only thought he was."

"Oh, I see! He came to life again?"

"I bet he didn't."

"Well, I never heard anything like this. *Somebody* was dead. *Somebody* was buried. Now, where was the mystery?"

"Ah! That's just it! That's it exactly. You see, we were twins . . . and we got mixed in the bathtub when we were only two weeks old, and one of us was drowned. But we didn't know which. Some think it was Bill. Some think it was me."

"Well, that is remarkable. What do you think?"

"Goodness knows! I would give whole worlds to know. This solemn, this awful tragedy has cast a gloom over my whole life. But I will tell you a secret now, which I never revealed to any creature before. One of us had a peculiar mark—a large mole on the back of his left hand; that was *me*. *That child was the one that was drowned!* . . ."

"I have an act I think you could use," the man said to the TV producer.

Out of one pocket he took a mouse and a miniature piano, which he placed on the producer's desk. Out of the other he took a beautiful butterfly. At once the mouse began to play and the butterfly began to sing.

"That is absolutely sensational," the producer said. "Name your price."

"Well," said the man, "there is one thing you should know. The act really isn't as good as it seems. You see, the butterfly can't sing. The mouse is a ventriloquist."

W hen Murgatroyd enlisted in the Navy he made practically perfect scores on all the tests they gave him. The officer who interviewed him was very impressed and asked what his occupation had been.

"Kluge maker," Murgatroyd replied.

The officer did not want to admit to such an extremely intelligent young man that he did not know what a kluge maker was. So he wrote down "kluge maker" on Murgatroyd's record.

Murgatroyd went through training camp with flying colors. When he was interviewed about his next assignment, he also told that officer that he had been a kluge maker. And that officer also did not want to admit that he had never heard of one.

"I'll make you a Kluge Maker First Class," he said. Of course, there is no such rating in the Navy, but with such an intelligent young man this seemed an exceptional case.

Murgatroyd was sent to Boston where he reported as a Kluge Maker First Class on the U.S.S. *Nymph,* which was going out on one of its first trips. It was a rugged trip, the weather was bad, and the crew really worked hard. But Murgatroyd just sat.

When they got back to Boston, the captain of the ship was pretty sore at him and accused him of not doing a thing the whole trip.

"Well," said Murgatroyd, "I'm a kluge maker. And I certainly couldn't make kluges without anything to make them with."

"What do you need?" asked the captain.

Murgatroyd sat up all night and made a long list—screws, bolts, hammers, axes, wire, batteries, iron, steel—the longest list you ever saw. They had to send all over to get the stuff. In fact, with the weight of all the kluge-making equipment, the ship leaned way to starboard when it went out again.

But Murgatroyd didn't do anything more on this trip than on the last one until the captain announced that the next morning an admiral would inspect the ship—and that the admiral was interested in kluges. The captain told Murgatroyd that he'd better have a kluge ready —or else.

When the admiral made his inspection the next morning he said to Murgatroyd, "I understand you have been making kluges."

"That's right, sir," Murgatroyd replied.

"Well, let's see one."

Murgatroyd opened his hand and there was the weirdest-looking thing you ever saw—with wires and springs sticking out in every direction.

Now the admiral had never seen a kluge before. But like the others he did not want to appear ignorant. He

coughed warily and said, "It looks like a perfect kluge. But if it's a perfect kluge, it should work perfectly. Let's see it work."

Murgatroyd walked straight to the side of the ship and dropped the kluge overboard.

And when it hit the water it went—Kkluuge!

# Notes
# Sources
# Bibliography

# ABBREVIATIONS IN
# NOTES, SOURCES, AND BIBLIOGRAPHY

BL     *Boys' Life*, "Think and Grin" columns
HF     *Hoosier Folklore*
HFB     *Hoosier Folklore Bulletin*
JA     Louis C. Jones Archives, New York State Historical Association, Cooperstown, N.Y. Folklore collected in the 1940s by students at Albany State Teachers College, N.Y., now Albany State College, under the direction of Professor Louis C. Jones.
JAF     *Journal of American Folklore*
KFR     *Kentucky Folklore Record*
LC     Library of Congress, Folk Song Section.
MF     *Midwest Folklore*
NYFQ     *New York Folklore Quarterly*
SFQ     *Southern Folklore Quarterly*
TA     Harold W. Thompson Archives, New York State Historical Association, Cooperstown, N.Y. Folklore collected in the 1940s and 1950s by Cornell University students under the direction of Professor Harold W. Thompson.
TFSB     *Tennessee Folklore Society Bulletin*
TXFS     Texas Folklore Society publication
UM     Maryland Folklore Archives, University of Maryland, College Park, Md.
WF     *Western Folklore*

# Notes

The publications cited are described in full in the bibliography.

*Witcracks:* I borrowed this from "a college of witcrackers," a term that Shakespeare used in *Much Ado About Nothing* to describe a group that spent much of its time cracking jokes. "Wisecrack" and "wisecracker" probably have the same ancestor or at least a close relative.

*When you . . . laugh* (p. 3): "Josh Billings" was a fellow named Henry Wheeler Shaw who turned to witcracking in the 1860s after trying his hand at farming, coal mining, exploring, and selling real estate in Poughkeepsie, New York.

*Jonathan, Jonathanism* (p. 17): "Brother Jonathan" is said to have been named for Governor Jonathan Trumbull of Connecticut, who during the Revolutionary War was a dependable source of supplies and advice. "We must consult Brother Jonathan" became a commonplace expression. And from Jonathan, as noted in the text, came the term "Jonathanism."

*The man with large feet* (p. 19): This Jonathanism appeared in a magazine published in the United States in 1858 (p. 113). In A.D. 77, Pliny the Elder, a famous writer and naturalist in ancient Rome, reported a similar wonder. In his book *Natural History* he described a mountain tribe in India whose members each had one leg and a foot so large its owner could lie on his back and, with the shade it cast, protect himself from the sun. See Polly Schoyer Brooks and Nancy Zinsser Walworth, *When the World Was Rome*, pp. 156–157.

*Elephant riddles* (p. 40): Although the early 1960s were the years of the elephant in the United States, Americans found them funny far earlier. At the turn of the century, people were asking why an elephant never goes visiting and explaining that he did not like to carry his trunk. And others were wondering why elephants and teapots were alike and pointing out that neither could climb a tree. See Mac E. Barrick, "The Shaggy Elephant Riddle," *SFQ* 28, pp. 266–290.

*The elephant in the cherry tree* (p. 42): In many related tales the goal is to protect oneself by keeping wild animals at a distance. The hero tries to do this by scattering bits of paper about, or sprinkling a special powder (such as lion powder) here and there, or simply snapping his fingers. When he is told he is wasting his time, that there aren't any wild animals nearby, often he replies: "See how effective it is!" But in another version told in the Soviet Union he responds: "Thank heavens! It's no good anyway." See Jan Harold Brunvand, "A Classification for Shaggy Dog Stories," *JAF* 76, pp. 42–68.

*Wellerisms* (p. 48): These expressions were at the height of their popularity in the United States from the 1830s through the 1860s when newspapers and humor magazines used them by the thousands. In those days they were also known as Yankeeisms, just as Jonathanisms were (p. 17). The few that remain in regular use are family sayings that have been handed down from generation to generation.

*Tom Swift* (p. 54): Tom Swift was the creation of Edward Stratemeyer, who wrote under the name Victor Appleton. When Tom finally retired and was replaced by Tom, Jr., Mr. Stratemeyer's daughter, Mrs. Harriet Adams, took over as Victor Appleton, Jr.

The ninety adventure stories father and daughter produced sold over 30 million copies, which perhaps helps explain why Tom Swifties so swiftly achieved their popularity. Actually, Tom was but one of the Stratemeyers' creations. There were also the Hardy Boys, the Rover Boys, the Bobbsey Twins, and, as one might expect, Nancy Drew who, just a few years ago, turned forty-two.

*Little Moron* (p. 59): Although Little Morons first appeared in the 1940s, they were the latest in an ancient line of noodles, numskulls, and other boobies that reached back in history to the ancient Chinese, Indians, Greeks, Sicilians, and other peoples.

Over the years, for unknown reasons a number of towns have become famous for their numskulls, even though they have no more than their fair share. One such place is Schildau in Germany. Others are Kampen in the Netherlands, Chelm in Poland, and Nol in Denmark. But the best known probably is Gotham in England which inspired this nursery rhyme:

> Three wise men of Gotham
> Went to sea in a bowl.
> If the bowl had been stronger,
> My song would be longer.

Many regions in the United States also have homegrown boobies. One example is *Jean Sot,* or Foolish John, in Louisiana. See Calvin Claudel, "Foolish John Tales from the French-Speaking Sections of Louisiana," *SFQ* 12, pp. 151–165.

No matter how ancient they may be or where they live, all numskulls behave the same way, at least in the tales that are told about them. The accounts of their experiences often are almost identical, even though thousands of years and miles may separate them.

Thus, the story of the boy and his father (p. 71) differs little from an ancient Turkish tale about a father who asks his son to guess what *he* has in his hand. The son guesses it is a millstone, which ordinarily is many feet across and often weighs a ton or more. See Paul Brewster, "Old Wine in New Bottles," *HFB* 3, p. 16.

Some years ago several children were asked to describe what a Little Moron looked like. It turned out that not one regarded him as a child. For a number he was a tall, skinny, middle-aged man in a hurry. For others he was "a little old guy" and "a regular jerk," with a black suit, a purple tie, and pigtails. See Martha Wolfenstein, *Children's Humor,* pp. 134–135.

*Insulting jokes* (p. 75): At one time or another most minority groups have been the targets of such jokes. When Irish immigrants began to arrive in the United States in the 1850s, a series of jokes about "Pat and Mike" developed. Some years later German immigrants were the target of "Hans and Fritz" jokes. Still later, Jews were the subject of stories that ridiculed their pronunciation of English.

Poor whites who have migrated to Ohio from the hill country in Kentucky and West Virginia, the section we call Appalachia, have received such treatment. Around Dayton, Ohio, for example, a series of "Briar" jokes have grown up about these people.* And curiously so has a series about their home states, particularly Kentucky.

One such joke goes: "I hear Cincinnati is expanding its zoo. They are building a fence around Kentucky." Another reports: "There was a fire in the governor's bathroom. But they put it out before it reached the house." See Clifford M. Stamper, "The Briar Joke in the Middle Miami Valley," *KFR* 15, pp. 35–36.

*Sut Lovingood* (p. 83): Lovingood was the creation of George Washington Harris, whose rough-hewn yarns were told in the dialect of the eastern Tennessee mountain people of the 1860s. Sut's specialty was practical jokes, one of which involved placing lizards in the trouser legs of a parson "while he is preachin' about the sarpints in hell." See Willard Thorp, *American Humorists*, p. 15.

*Willie, Audrey, and others* (pp. 84–87): If my sample is at all representative, Little Willie and Little Audrey continue to appeal to young people. But their humor is a world apart from the kinds of sick humor which have developed since the 1950s. This "new" humor deals with an array of subjects which earlier were rarely discussed, even in jokes.

In Brian Sutton-Smith's classic study of this genre, he cites as typical subjects the murder of friends and relatives, mutilation, cannibalism, indifference to children, disease and other afflictions, and religion, none of which formerly were regarded as funny, at

* "Briar" is a nickname for a Kentuckian.

least in public. See "'Shut Up and Keep Digging': The Cruel Joke Series," *MF* 10, pp. 11–22.

*Shaggy dog stories* (p. 89): The folklorist Jan Harold Brunvand has defined over two hundred kinds of shaggy dog tales, all of which depend on a punch line that is both unexpected and illogical. See *JAF* 76, pp. 42–68.

*Murgatroyd, the Kluge Maker* (p. 101–104): This tale is one of more than a dozen which follow the same pattern. Using many tools and much effort, the hero creates a weird object that in the end is good only for making an odd noise, which usually occurs only when it is dropped in water.

Along with "kkluuge," Brunvand cites "kush," "klesh," "gluck," "gleek," "ka-swish," "kloosch," "squish," "glug," "splooch," "blook," and "ding dong."

Lincoln told a story in the 1860s which involved a blacksmith who tried to make a sledgehammer and after several errors made a "fizz" by dropping the white-hot metal in a barrel of cold water. See Carl Sandburg, *Abraham Lincoln: The War Years*, vol. 4, p. 150.

Thirty years earlier Davy Crockett, then a member of the House of Representatives from Tennessee, used a similar story on the floor of Congress to attack a law another representative had proposed.

The story was about a neighbor of Crockett's who had tried to make an iron tool, but in the end he too gave up and heaved the hot metal into a barrel of water, where it went SKOW! "And . . . his bill will turn up a *skow*," Crockett warned. "Now mind if it don't." See William H. Jansen, "The Klesh-Maker," *HF* 7, p. 50.

# Sources

The source of each item is given, along with significant variants. The publications cited are described in full in the bibliography.

p. 3 *When you . . . laugh.* Quoted in Max Eastman, *Enjoyment of Laugher,* p. 331.

## 1.
## Last winter a cow nearby caught
## such a cold she gave nothing
## but ice cream.

p. 17 *Last winter a cow. Porter's Spirit of the Times,* New York, 6 (1859), p. 375.

*Jonathanisms.* Most of those cited appeared from 1840 to 1870 in publications in the United States. They are taken from an extensive index compiled by C. Grant Loomis, "Jonathanisms: American Epigrammatic Hyperbole," WF 6, pp. 211–217. A number have been adapted for clarity and brevity.

p. 18 *Who is so tall. Yankee Blade,* Boston, April 1, 1843.

*He has to get on his knees. California Spirit of the Times,* San Francisco, January 15, 1870.

*When he was born. Yankee Blade,* June 3, 1848.

*His shadow can't keep up. Yankee Blade,* December 31, 1842.

*His head grew three inches. Porter's Spirit of the Times* 6 (1859), no. 15.

p. 19 *Whose feet are so large. Ballou's Dollar Magazine* 8 (1858), p. 500.

p. 20 *There is a farmer who is so strong.* BL 22 (January, 1932), p. 45.

*He has a wife who is so clean.* Yankee Notions 11 (1862), p. 287.

p. 21 *It is so muddy.* Evan Esar, *The Humor of Humor,* p. 279.

p. 22 *It takes two of them to sneeze.* Porter's Spirit of the Times 3 (1858), p. 318.

*It takes two of them to chop wood.* Golden Era, San Francisco, 11 (1863), no. 2, p. 3.

p. 23 *Who is so dirty.* Yankee Notions 5 (1855), p. 71.

p. 24 *He put his cat to bed.* Oral tradition.

p. 25 *He put his best shirt to bed.* Yankee Blade, February 4, 1843.

*The buckwheat cake.* Daily Evening Transcript, Boston, November 12, 1835, quoting the *Advertiser,* Bangor, Maine.

## 2.
## What is yellow,
## smooth,
## and deadly?

p. 27 *What is yellow.* BL 62 (January, 1972), p. 84.
*Why can one never.* Oral tradition.

p. 28 *Why is that dog.* BL 54 (January, 1964), p. 58.
*Why did your cat.* BL 61 (March, 1971), p. 90.
*What did the five-hundred-pound.* Alta Jablow and Carl A. Withers, "Social Sense and Verbal Nonsense in Urban Children's Folklore," *NYFQ* 21, p. 251.

p. 30 *Why does the baby duck.* BL 44 (October, 1964), p. 64.
*Why does a cow.* Collected at Churchill Junior High School, East Brunswick, New Jersey, 1972.
*What did the cow ask.* JA, 1945.

p. 31 *What did the baby.* BL 40 (October, 1950), p. 66.

p. 32 *What is a boobee.* Ed Cray and Nancy C. Levanthal, "Depth Collecting from a Sixth Grade Class," *WF* 22, p. 254.

p. 33 *What did the angry.* BL 46 (May, 1956), p. 56.

p. 34 *What did one eye.* JA, 1945.
*What did one toe.* JA, 1945.
*What do you do.* Reported by Angella Reid, 12, Valley Road School, Princeton, New Jersey, 1973.
p. 35 *What is black and shiny.* Alta Jablow and Carl A. Withers, "Social Sense and Verbal Nonsense in Urban Children's Folklore," *NYFQ* 21, p. 251. Variants are reported in several archives, publications.
p. 36 *What is a ringleader.* BL 44 (April, 1954), p. 78.
p. 37 *And a meat thief.* BL 53 (February, 1963), p. 78.
*And a bulldozer.* BL 40 (September, 1950), p. 66.
*And rhubarb.* BL 62 (January, 1972), p. 84.
*And ignorance.* BL 21 (June, 1931), p. 47.
p. 38 *Little old lady.* Ed Cray and Nancy C. Levanthal, "Depth Collecting in a Sixth Grade Class," *WF* 22, p. 250.
*"Knock, knock" riddles.* Evan Esar, *The Humor of Humor.*
p. 39 *Cantaloupe.* Reported by Holly Light, 12, Andrea Hull, 12, Valley Road School, Princeton, New Jersey, 1973.
*Adolph.* Collected at Churchill Junior High School, East Brunswick, New Jersey, 1972.
*Sara.* LC, San Francisco, 1955.
*Dishes.* Martha Dirks, "Teen-Age Folklore from Kansas," *WF* 22, p. 98.
p. 40 *Why have a trunk.* UM, 1968. There are several variant responses, among them: "It can't afford a suitcase" (UM, 1968); "It doesn't have a glove compartment" (*BL* 53 [December, 1963], p. 78).
*Why have tusks.* UM, 1968.
*Why like peanuts.* UM, 1968.
*What is big and green.* Collected at Belmont School, Philadelphia, 1971. Also reported in Mac E. Barrick, "The Shaggy Elephant Riddle," *SFQ* 28, p. 270, as a joke used on "The Dick Van Dyke Show," WCBS-TV, November 20, 1963.
p. 41 *Why wear sneakers.* "Elephants by the Trunk," *Time* 82 (August 2, 1963), p. 41.
*What goes clomp, clomp.* BL 61 (September, 1971), p. 90.
p. 42 *Why does an elephant paint.* Alta Jablow and Carl A.

Withers, "Social Sense and Verbal Nonsense in Urban Children's Folklore," *NYFQ* 21, p. 250. Adapted slightly for clarity.

*How does an elephant get.* UM, Mary Lee Burbage, 1968.

*How does he get out.* Various publications, archives.

p. 43 *How can you tell when.* Collected at Churchill Junior High School, East Brunswick, New Jersey, 1972; Rutgers University, New Brunswick, New Jersey, 1972. A variant, "You're close to the ceiling," collected in Pennsylvania, is reported by Mac E. Barrick in "The Shaggy Elephant Riddle," *SFQ* 28, p. 274. Also attributed by Barrick to Marcie Hans and Lynn Babcock, *There's an Elephant in My Sandwich,* a book published in 1963.

p. 44 *What is the best way.* UM, 1968.

*How do you stop.* UM, 1968.

*Why short pants.* UM, 1968.

p. 45 *Why sunglasses.* UM, John Diver, 1967.

## 3.
## I bought a wooden whistle,
## but it wooden whistle.

p. 47 *Oliver Wendell Holmes.* Quoted in Max Eastman, "What We Laugh At and Why," *Reader's Digest,* April, 1966, p. 66.

p. 48 *This is r-r-r-rough.* Reported by Nancy Fish, 13, Concord, Massachusetts, 1972.

*This can't be beat. Yankee Blade,* April 23, 1844. Quoted in C. Grant Loomis, "Traditional American Word Play: Wellerisms or Yankeeisms," *WF* 7, p. 4.

*Wellerisms.* See C. Grant Loomis, *WF* 7, pp. 1–21, which classifies some four hundred Wellerisms in use from 1840 to 1870; Loomis, "Wellerisms in California Sources," *WF* 14, pp. 229–245, which includes an additional three hundred dating to 1855; Herbert Halpert, "Some Wellerisms from Kentucky and Tennessee," *JAF* 69, pp. 115–122; and William E. Koch,

"Wellerisms from Kansas," *WF* 18, p. 180, and "More Wellerisms from Kansas," *WF* 19, p. 196.

p. 49 *I believe in getting.* Family tradition. In Loomis, *WF* 7, p. 6, a schoolmarm and one of her pupils are the participants.

p. 50 *I'm all in.* The Pelican [a student publication at the University of California, Berkeley] 16, no. 4. Quoted in Loomis, *WF* 14, p. 237.

*I have a pressing.* Halpert, *JAF* 69, p. 118.

*This is the end.* Halpert, *JAF* 69, p. 117.

p. 51 *So long.* Koch, *WF* 18, p. 180.

p. 52 *Man who put face in.* BL 61 (April, 1971), p. 74.

*Chemist who fall in. Senior Scholastic* 69 (March 18, 1940), p. 35.

*Man who live in.* BL 58 (August, 1968), p. 62.

*Place to look for.* BL 62 (April, 1972), p. 84.

p. 53 *Man who put foot.* BL 61 (February, 1971), p. 78.

p. 54 *I'll have four hot dogs.* BL 53 (September, 1963), p. 86.

*I have just inherited.* UM, 1968.

*I'll have two sodas.* UM, 1968.

*What vegetable.* UM, 1968.

p. 55 *Whoops.* BL 61 (August, 1971), p. 66.

*Please pass.* Reported by Kathy Boonin, 12, Valley Road School, Princeton, New Jersey, 1973.

*I don't have.* UM, 1968.

p. 56 *Have you heard.* BL 53 (August, 1963), p. 62.

p. 57 *I bought.* BL 44 (September, 1955), p. 64.

## 4.
## "I snored so loud
## I used to wake myself up."

p. 59 *I snored so loud.* BL 22 (November, 1932), p. 36.

p. 60 *This house painter.* Various publications, archives.

p. 62 *I weighed only three.* An old vaudeville joke reported by Rudolph Umland, "The Demise of the Little Moron," *Esquire* 20, p. 155.

*I'm really glad.* Various archives, publications, in which

Egbert also is Willie, Jimmy, and Sam.
*This woman's son.* TA, 1945.

p. 63 *After everyone was.* I learned this as a graduate student at Northwestern University, 1950. A variant is reported in Ernest W. Baughman, "Little Moron Stories," *HFB* 2, p. 17.

p. 64 *A crew of workmen.* Rudolph Umland, "The Demise of the Little Moron," *Esquire* 20, p. 155.

p. 66 *The man who threw.* TA, 1945.
*The girl who went.* TA, 1945.
*The boy who sat.* TA, 1945.
*The family who moved.* TA, 1945.

p. 67 *The boy who thought.* TA, 1945.
*The girl who was.* TA, 1945.

p. 68 *The football player.* TA, 1945.
*The man who went.* TA, 1945.
*The man who wore.* TA, 1945.

p. 69 *The girl who tied.* Reported by my students at Rutgers University, New Brunswick, N.J., and by my wife's at Churchill Junior High School, East Brunswick, N.J., 1973. Thirty years earlier an almost identical account was included in Levette Jay Davidson, "Moron Stories," *SFQ* 7, p. 104.

p. 70 *A boy and his father.* I learned this as a graduate student at Northwestern University, 1950. A variant is reported in Paul Brewster, "Old Wine in New Bottles," *HFB* 3, no. 1, p. 16.

p. 72 *Why did the girl.* TA, 1945.

p. 73 *Three boys were sharing.* One of my students at Rutgers University told me this story in 1972. Herbert Halpert reports a similar version in "More About the Little Moron," *HFB* 2, p. 49.

## 5.
## Ahs your new neighbor.

p. 76, 77 *Why do flies.* This item and the seven that follow were reported by my sons, John, 18, and Peter, 16, who learned them at Princeton, New Jersey, High School and at summer camps in the northeastern United States, and by students at Rutgers University, 1973. For variants see Donald C. Simmons, "Anti-Italian-American Riddles in New England," *JAF* 79, pp. 475–478.

p. 78 *White milk* and *white shoes.* Langston Hughes, "Jokes Negroes Tell on Themselves," *Negro Digest* 9, p. 21. Adapted slightly for clarity.

*My daddy got that one.* Hughes, *Negro Digest* 9, p. 22. Adapted slightly for clarity.

p. 79 *Don't you see.* Carl Sandburg. *The Sandburg Range,* p. 372. Excerpted from *Abraham Lincoln: The Prairie Years.*

*Ahs your new neighbor.* Langston Hughes, *The Book of Negro Humor,* p. 262.

*The two copilots.* Joseph Boskin, "Good-by, Mr. Bones," *New York Times Magazine,* May 1, 1966, p. 92. Adapted slightly for clarity.

p. 80 *Good heavens, Tonto.* Isaac Asimov, *Isaac Asimov's Treasury of Humor,* p. 295.

p. 81 *Eateateat.* Asimov, p. 259. Adapted slightly for clarity.

## 6.
## "Johnny, stop twisting
## your sister's head."

p. 83 *Johnny, stop twisting.* Brian Sutton-Smith, " 'Shut Up and Keep Digging': The Cruel Joke Series," *MF* 10, p. 13.

p. 84 *Billy in one of.* D. Streamer, *Ruthless Rhymes for Heartless Homes,* quoted in Evan Esar, *The Humor of Humor,* p. 281.

*Little Willie with.* Childhood recollection from Delmar, New York, 1930s, reported by Barbara Carmer Schwartz, Princeton, New Jersey, 1973. A variant is reported in "Bloody Mary, Anyone?" *Time* 35 (October 21, 1957), p. 27.

*Willie fell down.* Evan Esar, *The Humor of Humor,* p.

281. Adapted slightly for clarity.

p. 85 *Trucks and steamrollers* and *parachute lessons.* Childhood recollection from Delmar, New York, 1930s, reported by Barbara Carmer Schwartz, Princeton, New Jersey, 1973. A variant of the "trucks and steamrollers" tale is reported in Ed Cray and Nancy C. Leventhal, "Depth Collecting from a Sixth Grade Class," *WF* 22, p. 250. For variant of the "parachute lessons" tale see Cornelia Chambers, "The Adventures of Little Audrey," *TXFS* 13, p. 107, a major collection of Audrey material.

p. 86 *Why are we out.* Reported by Peter Schwartz, 16, Princeton, New Jersey. Learned at Camp Wanderlust, Molonkus, Maine, 1972. A variant is reported in Brian Sutton-Smith, "'Shut Up and Keep Digging': The Cruel Joke Series," *MF* 10, p. 13.

*I don't want to go.* Reported by Peter Schwartz, 16. Variants are reported in Brian Sutton-Smith, *MF* 10, p. 17, and Martha Dirks, "Teen-Age Folklore from Kansas," *WF* 22, p. 92.

*Garbage disposal.* Brian Sutton-Smith, *MF* 10, p. 17.

*Bake cookies.* Ed Cray and Nancy C. Leventhal, "Depth Collecting from a Sixth Grade Class," *WF* 22, p. 250.

*Running so fast.* Students at Rutgers University, 1973. Variants are reported in Martha Dirks, "Teen-Age Folklore from Kansas," *WF* 22, p. 91, and Roger D. Abrahams, "Ghastly Commands: The Cruel Joke Revisited," *MF* 11, p. 244.

p. 87 *World War III joke.* Alta Jablow and Carl A. Withers, "Social Sense and Verbal Nonsense in Urban Children's Folklore," *NYFQ* 21, p. 252.

## 7.
### Kkluuge!

p. 89 *The dog got lost.* Oral tradition. For detailed index of shaggy dog tales, see Jan Harold Brunvand, "A Classification for Shaggy Dog Stories," *JAF* 76, pp. 42–68.

p. 90 *A city man named Smith.* BL 47 (February, 1957), p. 78. Retold from a synopsis.

p. 91 *A reindeer walked.* BL 42 (October, 1952), p. 74.

p. 92 *The Horse That Sat on Grapefruit.* J. C. Furnas, "Don't Laugh Now," *Esquire* 5, p. 56. Retold from a synopsis. A variant, "The Horse Who Sat on Eggs," is reported in Donald Ogden Stewart, *The Crazy Fool,* pp. 148–151. Both are descendants of an anecdote Abraham Lincoln told about a man who sold a horse that was good not only for hunting birds but for catching fish. See Carl Sandburg, *Abraham Lincoln: The Prairie Years,* vol. 2, p. 300.

p. 94 *There was this knight.* BL 45 (January, 1955), p. 63. Retold from a synopsis.

p. 95 *On this island lived.* BL 55 (November, 1965), p. 86. Retold from a synopsis.

p. 96 *An elderly man.* BL 42 (September, 1952), p. 74. Adapted slightly for clarity. Eric Partridge reports an elaborate variant in *The "Shaggy Dog" Story: Its Origin, Development, and Nature (With a Few Seemly Examples),* p. 90.

p. 98 *A story Mark Twain once told.* Quoted in Henri Bergson, *Laughter: An Essay on the Meaning of the Comic,* p. 191. Adapted slightly for clarity.

p. 100 *I have an act.* BL 53 (December, 1963), p. 96. Adapted for clarity.

p. 101 *Murgatroyd, the Kluge Maker.* Reported in Agnes Nolan Underwood, "Folklore from G.I. Joe," *NYFQ* 3, pp. 295–297. Portions have been adapted to reduce length.

# Bibliography

## Books

Books that may be of particular interest to young people are marked with an asterisk ( * ).

Asimov, Isaac. *Isaac Asimov's Treasury of Humor.* Boston: Houghton Mifflin Company, 1971.

Bergson, Henri. *Laughter: An Essay on the Meaning of the Comic.* Translated by Cloudesley Bereton and Fred Rothwell. London: The Macmillan Company, 1921.

Bier, Jesse. *The Rise and Fall of American Humor.* New York: Holt, Rinehart & Winston, 1968.

* Blake, Robert, ed. *101 Elephant Jokes.* New York: Scholastic Book Services, 1964.

* Bontemps, Arna, and Hughes, Langston, eds. *The Book of Negro Folklore.* New York: Dodd, Mead & Company, 1958.

* Botkin, Benjamin A. *A Treasury of American Folklore.* New York: Crown Publishers, 1944.

* Brooks, Polly Schoyer, and Walworth, Nancy Zinsser. *When the World Was Rome.* New York: J. B. Lippincott Company, 1972.

Clouston, W. A. *The Book of Noodles.* London: Elliot Stock, 1888. *A classic collection of noodle and numskull tales.*

Dundes, Alan, ed. *Mother Wit from the Laughing Barrel: Readings in the Interpretation of Afro-American Folklore.* Englewood Cliffs, N.J.: Prentice-Hall, Inc., 1973.

Eastman, Max. *Enjoyment of Laughter.* New York: Simon and Schuster, 1936. Reprint edition, New York: Johnson Reprint Corporation, 1970.

Esar, Evan. *The Humor of Humor.* New York: Horizon Press, 1952.

Harris, George Washington. *Sut Lovingood's Yarns.* New York: Dick & Fitzgerald, 1867.

Hughes, Langston, ed. *The Book of Negro Humor.* New York: Dodd, Mead & Company, 1966.

Koestler, Arthur. *The Act of Creation.* New York: The Macmillan Company, 1967.

————. *Insight and Outlook: An Inquiry into the Common Foundations of Science, Art, and Social Ethics.* New York: The Macmillan Company, 1949.

* Leach, Maria. *Noodles, Nitwits, and Numskulls.* Cleveland and New York: The World Publishing Company, 1961. *A most pleasant introduction to the noodle tale.*

* ————. *Riddle Me, Riddle Me, Ree.* New York: The Viking Press, 1970.

Partridge, Eric. *The "Shaggy Dog" Story: Its Origin, Development and Nature (With a Few Seemly Examples).* New York: Philosophical Library, 1954.

Ranke, Kurt, ed. *European Anecdotes and Jests.* Copenhagen: Rosenkilde & Bagger, 1972.

* Rourke, Constance. *American Humor: A Study of the National Character.* New York: Harcourt, Brace & Company, 1931. *Perhaps the finest account of early American humor.*

Sandburg, Carl. *Abraham Lincoln: The Prairie Years.* 2 vols. New York: Harcourt, Brace & Company, 1926.

————.*Abraham Lincoln: The War Years.* 4 vols. New York: Harcourt, Brace & Company, 1939.

* ————. *The Sandburg Range.* New York: Harcourt, Brace & Company, 1957.

*Standard Dictionary of Folklore, Mythology, and Legend.* Edited by Maria Leach. 2 vols. New York: Funk & Wagnalls, 1949.

Sterling, Philip. *Laughing on the Outside: The Intelligent White Reader's Guide to Negro Tales and Humor.* New York: Grosset & Dunlap, 1965.

Stewart, Donald Ogden. *The Crazy Fool.* New York: Albert & Charles Boni, 1925.

Streamer, D. [pseud. of Graham, Henry]. *Ruthless Rhymes for Heartless Homes.* London: E. Arnold, 1899(?).

Taylor, Archer. *The Proverb.* Cambridge, Massachusetts: Harvard University Press, 1931.

Thorp, Willard. *American Humorists.* Minneapolis: University of Minnesota Press, 1964.

* Tidwell, James N., ed. *A Treasury of American Folk Humor.* New York: Crown Publishers, 1956.

Wolfenstein, Martha. *Children's Humor.* Glencoe, Illinois: The Free Press, 1954. *A psychoanalytic study.*

Zewbskewiecz, Jerome, *et al. It's Fun to Be a Polack.* Glendale, California: Collectors Publications, Inc., 1965.

## Articles

Abrahams, Roger D. "The Bigger They Are, the Harder They Fall." *TFSB* 29 (1963):94–102.

————. "Ghastly Commands: The Cruel Joke Revisited." *MF* 11 (1961):235–246.

Barrick, Mac E. "The Shaggy Elephant Riddle." *SFQ* 28 (1964):266–290. *A classification.*

Baughman, Ernest W. "Little Moron Stories." *HFB* 2 (1941): 17–18.

Boskin, Joseph. "Good-by, Mr. Bones." *New York Times Magazine,* May 1, 1966, pp. 31, 92.

Brewster, Paul. "Old Wine in New Bottles." *HFB* 3 (1944): 16–22. *A comparison of Little Moron stories and early noodle tales.*

Brunvand, Jan Harold. "A Classification for Shaggy Dog Stories." *JAF* 76 (1963):42–68.

Burma, John H. "Humor as a Technique in Race Conflict." *American Sociological Review* 11 (1946):710–715.

Chambers, Cornelia. "The Adventures of Little Audrey." *Straight Texas,* TXFS 13 (1937):106–110.

Claudel, Calvin. "Foolish John Tales from the French-Speaking Sections of Louisiana." *SFQ* 12 (1948):151–165.

"Confucius Say . . ." *Senior Scholastic* 69 (March, 1940), p. 35.

Cray, Ed, and Leventhal, Nancy C. "Depth Collecting from a Sixth Grade Class." *WF* 22 (1963):159–163, 231–257.

Davidson, Levette Jay. "Moron Stories." *SFQ* 7 (1943):101–104.

Dirks, Martha. "Teen-Age Folklore from Kansas." *WF* 22 (1963):89–102.

Dresser, Norine. "The Metamorphosis of the Humor of the Black Man." *NYFQ* 26 (1970):216–228.

Dundes, Alan. "The Elephant Joking Question." *TFSB* 29 (1963):40–41.

Furnas, J. C. "Don't Laugh Now." *Esquire* 5 (May, 1937), pp. 56, 236.

Halpert, Herbert. "More About the Little Moron." *HFB* 2:49.

————. "Some Wellerisms from Kentucky and Tennessee." *JAF* 69 (1956):115–122.

Hughes, Langston. "Jokes Negroes Tell on Themselves." *Negro Digest* 9 (June, 1951), pp. 21–25.

Jablow, Alta, and Withers, Carl A. "Social Sense and Verbal Nonsense in Urban Children's Folklore." *NYFQ* 21 (1965): 243–257.

Jansen, William H. "The Klesh-Maker." *HF* 7 (1948):47–50.

Koch, William E. "More Wellerisms from Kansas." *WF* 19 (1960):196.

————. "Wellerisms from Kansas." *WF* 18 (1959):180.

Loomis, C. Grant. "Jonathanisms: American Epigrammatic Hyperbole." *WF* 6 (1947):211–227. *An index, 1830–1860.*

————. "Traditional American Word Play: Wellerisms or Yankeeisms." *WF* 7 (1948):1–21. *An index, 1840–1870.*

————. "Wellerisms in California Sources." *WF* 14 (1955): 229–245. *An index, 1855–1945.*

Porter, Kenneth. "Some Central Kansas Wellerisms." *MF* 8 (1958):158–160.

Simmons, Donald C. "Anti-Italian-American Riddles in New England." *JAF* 79 (1966):475–478.

Sims, Dunny. "Moron Jokes." *From Hell to Breakfast,* TXFS 19 (1944):155–161.

Stamper, Clifford M. "The Briar Joke in the Middle Miami Valley." *KFR* 15 (1969):35–36.

Sutton-Smith, Brian. " 'Shut Up and Keep Digging': The Cruel Joke Series." *MF* 10 (1960):11–22. *An index.*

Taylor, Archer. "Wellerisms." *Standard Dictionary of Folklore, Mythology, and Legend,* vol. 2, pp. 1169–1170.

————. "Wellerisms and Riddles." *WF* 19 (1960):55.

"Think and Grin" columns of jokes. *Boys' Life,* vols. 1–63 (1919–1973).

Umland, Rudolph. "The Demise of the Little Moron." *Esquire* 20 (September, 1943), pp. 32–35.

Underwood, Agnes Nolan. "Folklore from G.I. Joe." *NYFQ* 3 (1947):285–297.

Welch, Roger L. "American Numskull Tales: The Polack Joke." *WF* 26 (1967):183–186.

# An Acknowledgment

The following persons and organizations helped me create this book:

Professor Bruce R. Buckley of the Cooperstown, N.Y., Graduate Programs, who made it possible for me to study the holdings of the folklore archives at the New York State Historical Association, and Mrs. Marion Brophey, the librarian in charge of special collections, who served as my guide.

Professor Esther K. Birdsall, Mrs. Geraldine Johnson, and Nathan Olivera of the University of Maryland, who made materials available at the Maryland Folklore Archives.

Professor Kenneth S. Goldstein of the University of Pennsylvania, who placed his personal library of folklore at my disposal and was helpful in many other ways.

The folklore students whose research I was privileged to review. My students at Rutgers University who over the years have contributed to my folklore collections.

The children at Valley Road and John Witherspoon schools in Princeton, New Jersey; those at Churchill Junior High School in East Brunswick, New Jersey; and those at Belmont School, Philadelphia, who shared their jokes with me.

Peter, Nancy, and Elizabeth Schwartz, who reviewed the thousands of jokes and jests I collected and helped me decide which would appeal most to other young people.

Librarians at Princeton University, Rutgers University, the University of Maine, the Princeton, New Jersey, Public Library, and the national headquarters of the Boy Scouts of America.

The folklorists, folklore journals, folklore societies, and publishing firms which permitted me to include various materials. I am grateful to each.

A. S.

## ABOUT ALVIN SCHWARTZ

Alvin Schwartz has written many books for young people and for families on subjects as varied as folklore, crafts, hobbies, museums, labor unions, and urban problems. He works in a tiny studio in Princeton, New Jersey, next to the house where he lives with his wife, four children, and two cats.

## ABOUT GLEN ROUNDS

Glen Rounds spent his childhood on ranches in South Dakota and Montana. He attended art school in Kansas City, Missouri, and in New York City, and now lives in Southern Pines, North Carolina. He has written and illustrated many books for young people.

*Also by Alvin Schwartz and Glen Rounds*

A Twister of Twists, A Tangler of Tongues
Tomfoolery: Trickery and Foolery with Words